Coming Back
To Myself

A Compassionate Guide to Understanding and Healing from an Eating Disorder

"The book I wish I had when I was struggling."
- Someone in recovery

Maria Ortiz, MS, LMHC, CEDS

Published by:
BreakFree Therapy Services, LLC
Fort Myers, FL

ISBN: 979-8-9939091-1-0

Printed in the United States of America
First Edition, 2025

From The Author

I am personally recovered from an eating disorder and am now a Certified Eating Disorder Specialist and Licensed Mental Health Counselor. I struggled for many years through many behaviors and many severities. I hope this book can be the perfect blend of insights from my lived experience and professional expertise. My goals for writing this book are to help inspire individuals with an eating disorder to believe they can recover, to give them some starting ideas and perspectives to take the next step, and to provide those supporting individuals with an eating disorder with more information and understanding of what's behind the diagnosis. I also hope to validate and acknowledge that these disorders are so damaging, all-consuming, and truly a nightmare to live through, while also instilling hope for "after."

I know what it feels like to live through an eating disorder, and I know how to treat individuals struggling with one from a therapeutic lens. Here's to hoping this combination can help even one person on the road to recovery. You deserve to find your freedom.

Disclosure

This book is not intended to replace therapy, nor is its content considered a therapeutic recommendation. This book is intended for educational and informational purposes only. It is not a substitute for professional mental health care, diagnosis, or treatment. Readers should seek the guidance of qualified health professionals regarding any mental health concerns, including eating disorders. The author and publisher disclaim any liability for any adverse consequences or damages resulting from the use of the information contained in this book. The author assumes no fault or liability for engagement with the ideas in this book or for potential outcomes. This book was written with the best intentions as a possible aid in someone's journey alongside professional help and recommendations.

If you are struggling with an eating disorder, please reach out to a mental health provider today and meet with your doctor as soon as possible. Call 911 or go to a local emergency room if experiencing any potential life-threatening or physical symptoms associated with an eating disorder or mental health concern. If applicable, the author recommends following your specific treatment team's plan and interventions, while using this book as a supportive tool. If you do not already have a treatment team, the author hopes this book can inspire courage and motivation to seek professional help and to reach out to your loved ones and professionals for support during this time. Eating disorders are deadly disorders, and warrant attention and treatment from a multidisciplinary treatment team of professionals, including but not limited to:

- Therapist/Psychologist
- Registered Dietitian
- Primary Care Physician
- Psychiatry Professional
- Other Specialty Medical Doctors as needed

This book is not intended nor recommended to be a stand-alone support. The author recommends seeking professional support.

Table of Contents

Message of Hope

If you had told me years ago that I'd be an eating disorder therapist, I never would've believed you. In fact, I would have outright laughed for these reasons:

1) I had my life planned out; After all, I thought I had it all under my complete control. I was going to become a Physician Assistant. I was going to be "skinny" while attaining this. Nothing else mattered, and there were no alternatives.

2) I initially didn't believe in therapy. I didn't feel I was sick. I thought I just ate "different" than others. I thought I was just a dedicated athlete with "normal" body image concerns. Who am I to become an ED therapist?

3) Once I accepted that I was sick, I never pictured myself getting better. Let this be a motivation to you: I insisted I'd never recover, that I'd never enjoy a life with food, that I'd never be happy in a larger body than the one I was in, that no one understood my pain, that my struggle was "different," that treatment wouldn't work for me, that this would be my life forever.

Boy, was I wrong.

I struggled for many years. In the early days, my eating
disorder would've fit what we now call ARFID
(Avoidant/Restrictive Food Intake Disorder), though this term
was not popularized nor acknowledged during this time.
Eventually, my struggles shifted into behaviors relating to
weight and body shape. This included restriction, different
purging methods, and over-exercising. I initially mastered
keeping my illness a secret. I'd make sure to eat enough in front
of others to avoid raising alarm, blame my exercise on my
dedication to my sport, and take every measure to keep purging
behaviors secret.

During the early years, people complimented my body.
They complimented my thinness, my strength, and my overall
frame. "You're so tall and skinny!" is a sentence I heard pretty
often. This ingrained these qualities into my identity, more than
I knew at the time. "Wow, you have so much willpower!" rang
from people's mouths as I'd turn down yummy foods and make
the "healthiest" choice available. It was like this secret I kept
made me inherently so powerful. No one knew what was going
on in my head, and that initially felt so magical. I felt like I had
accomplished something each time I pulled a fast one over those
around me and successfully lied for another day. While my

body looked societally idealistic, the world around me praised my behaviors, with no insight into the damage I was doing.

What will forever interest me, that I carry into my work, is that the voices of concern did not come until I "looked" sick. The reason this was so perplexing to me was that my behaviors and mindset had not changed; Only my body had. Once specific amounts of weight loss were "concerning" to others, it's like suddenly people thought something was wrong. I wasn't receptive to this concern because nothing had changed to me besides my body, yet *now* what I was doing was a problem? The way I handle this occurrence in my work is that I give minimal merit to body size or weight. I keep in mind that so much of this disorder can't be seen, and I try not to be another voice that validates the notion of "once you look sick, people care." I've found that this is one of the toughest things for people to understand: That the manner in which someone is struggling may completely contradict their visual "look."

I cannot tell you how many times people assumed I was recovered due to achieving weight restoration. From doctors to therapists alike, it's as if my weight increase signaled to them that I was "okay now." They *said* they understood that I was still struggling, yet their words and actions no longer met what their old concern used to look and feel like.

They *said* they knew I was still in pain, but their check-ins and appointments decreased.

They *assured me* they still took my struggles seriously, yet they stopped assessing for my use of behaviors.

They told me, "The rest will take time," and congratulated me on my progress.

Didn't they know I was still dying inside?

I find it interesting how few people know that just because someone gains weight doesn't mean they're better. However, people seem to understand this when it comes to addictions. When someone is sober, everyone acknowledges the challenges they will continue to face and the turmoil that is within to fight their thoughts and urges consistently. Where is this energy for eating disorders? Additionally, let's all remember that not everyone with an ED will even lose weight.

Through weight changes and behavior shifts, there were a few components of my eating disorder that I found to be the most detrimental. They are the same components I see consistently wreak havoc in my clients' lives. The top 10 components I'd like to highlight are:

1) Hopelessness

2) Worry Feels Like Love

3) Anosognosia

4) Relentless Thoughts

5) Feeling Alone

6) Addictiveness

7) Competition

8) Lying

9) Secrecy

10) Losing Yourself

If you want to understand more about or heal from an eating disorder, you must recognize how these components together can impact a quality of life, how these mechanisms present, and how to adequately fight them.

Hopelessness

There are many reasons I'm choosing to speak first about the experience of hopelessness. The most imperative being, that I firmly believe it's why this disorder keeps people sick for so long, or even ends their life. I believe it is an eating disorder's most potent weapon. After all, why should people fight for recovery if they don't think it's possible? Why should they give it their all when their ED says day after day that they'll never get better? Who fights with no hope in what you're fighting for?

I always ask my clients, "If I could guarantee you that you'd be living a life in true recovery within the next 4 years, would it make you fight harder? Would you approach your recovery efforts differently?" More than 9 times out of 10, I am met with the answer that aligns with something of the sort of, "Well, of course, if it were guaranteed!" What this illustrates to me is that an individual believing that they can get better is imperative to proper and total engagement in the recovery process. Let's also acknowledge how this hopelessness intertwines with depressive symptoms. How is one supposed to feel optimistic about their life and future without the belief that things will ever get better?

I also believe that hopelessness is one of the most significant indicators of a potential relapse or overall regression in recovery. Without hope, there comes a time in a recovery process where the individual must ask themselves the question, "I can't guarantee that my efforts will pay off. *Do I keep going or do I turn back?*" I notice this decision primarily pops up around the time when weight restoration is completing, when weight restoration is initially being maintained, or when nutrition has sufficiently improved or increased. People often express, "Okay, I did the work. I gained weight. I eat more now."

"Am I just supposed to hate myself forever?"

Now, this is the time that if the individual doesn't have hope... hope that their body image improves, hope that this process works, hope that their re-nourishment leads to cognitive improvement... they will turn around.

"I'd rather hate myself and be skinny rather than hate myself and be 'fat.'"

Not only have I heard other individuals express this sentiment, but it's also one I recall saying myself. We *know* re-nourishment is needed for appropriate cognitive progress to occur. But, wow, it is a challenging experience to tolerate while that happens. Here's what I say to my clients: No, I cannot guarantee these improvements will 100% lead to the desired outcome. However, I do *know* that going backwards won't achieve your goals either. Say, you go backwards; You return to safety through behavior use or weight loss (if part of your story). Then what? You will *have* to retake these steps to get you right back to this exact place: the decision to move forward or return to the ED again. Someday, you will take the risk, and this particular risk is terrifying. However, this same risk comes with the possibility of getting you to the rest of your life: Is it worth it? Please don't let your ED answer that question; Maybe let your inner child answer it instead. Take the step before you're *ready*, as the ED will probably never allow you to experience that feeling. It's much too smart for that... and it doesn't want to lose you.

I have a fascinating perspective on how the power of hope influences therapeutic improvement. I vividly remember having no hope that my life could get better. I would try to explain to every professional/provider I met that they didn't understand that recovery just "wasn't possible" for me. I believed it 100% that I could not get better. There was not a consideration of "What if?" but rather an unrelenting *knowledge* that recovery would never be achieved for me.

Here are a few illustrative sentences I recall saying with my entire chest, and believing with everything in me:

"I will never accept a body that society calls healthy."

"I will never have a day where my first thought isn't my body size or weight."

"I will never allow my body to fluctuate through life the way others' do."

"I will never allow myself to eat what I want without regard for how my body could change."

"I will never let go of my thin identity. It's the most important thing in my life."

"I've struggled for most of my life; My brain is not capable of recovery due to it accommodating my disorder for the majority of my life."

"I'll never recover, because then all of this was 'for nothing.' I would never throw in the towel now."

"I'll never let the people in my life see me gain weight."

"I don't want recovery. I value my perfectionism."

"Nobody understands that I'm not like other clients. My ED does not have the capacity to let up."

I could go on and on with sentences that illustrate just how serious I was about my belief relating to being sick for the remainder of my life. After all, these sentences were my world for many years. I share these with a few intentions:

1) To know that you're not alone if you also have these thoughts.
2) To show individuals who haven't struggled just how real these thoughts feel at the time.
3) To show just how much progress someone can make, no matter where their starting line is.

After all, I believed these thoughts wholeheartedly, and now have gone many, many years living a fully recovered life. In all honesty, it's tough to picture myself having those thoughts now. I've often gotten the question, "Doesn't working with individuals with eating disorders trigger you?" My answer always seems to surprise people, and it is this: When I first decided to go into this field specifically, I did share this concern. I thought and believed I was in a strong recovery, but I had a rightful worry about whether seeing individuals struggling could ever cause countertransference for me, in the manner of maybe over-identifying with my clients, being reminded of my own journey, or even triggering old thoughts and ways.

On the contrary, I have found it incredibly challenging and requires intention to get back in touch with my old self. It feels like a different version of me was alive during that time that isn't here now. I always try to approach my work with grace, but I've caught myself many times saying, "Maria, let's remember how challenging this really was." What I'm saying is, I often forget that this was my life; that this is a part of my story. It feels so far away, and downright impossible that I felt that way, engaged with the behaviors I did, and lived through that struggle.

Moral of the story: Never underestimate how far you can go, and how far recovery can bring you. I lacked any belief in my ability to live an even *better* life; yet here I am, living a life where I have to *intentionally try* to reconnect with my old self to understand what those in my practice may be going through. Though I keep a professional boundary and lens,

I do find value in reminding myself of just how hard the fight my clients are facing is. If you're reading this book, please know that I know. I know what it feels like to insist you'll never get better. I know how it feels to wake up every morning and hop on the scale, with no hope for when that cycle will ever end. I know what it feels like to feel different; to feel wholeheartedly like though recovery may be possible for others, it isn't for you. I know what it feels like to go through life hopeless. I'm here to remind you: This is a weapon of your disorder, not a reality.

I relate it to that and those who struggle with suicide. People wouldn't take their own lives if they had the genuine belief that life would improve. They take their life because they are *hopeless about* the notion that things will ever get better. Please remind yourself of this. Depression and eating disorders say you won't ever get better for a significant reason: You won't fight for a future that is hopeless to improve. This is *intentionally* used to cause harm. Once you can remember this is a weapon, not an actual thought from within yourself, you have something to fight with and to fight for. Let this be the reminder that I tell all my clients:

I would never do this job if I didn't honestly believe that recovery is possible. It would be the most unpleasant job in the world to watch people struggle in the manner to which I believe is one of the worst things one could ever go through-not ever to see many get better. Don't get me wrong, I don't do this job strictly for the good days when someone gets their life back. I also have so much gratitude to be able to walk along individuals' paths with them while the road is still dark, gloomy, and *seemingly* hopeless. I do this job because I have the utmost belief that people can fight this disorder and deserve to live a life that's truly worth living. I can be the bearer of hope until my clients can feel it for themselves.

Worry Feels Like Love

In complete transparency, I did always feel loved by my family and friends. I never questioned or wavered on their love for me. With this being said, eating disorders have a magnificent way of convincing humans that they've found home in that worry is the most expressive and obvious form of love and care.

"Is everything okay?"

"Do you need a check-in?"

"Please keep fighting; I'll fight with you."

"I'm worried about you."

"I'm scared for you."

"Did you eat today?"

"What do you need?"

"How can I help?"

"I'm praying for you."

"Know I'm always here for you."

"Just tell me what to do, and I'll do it."

"Do you need a ride to your appointment?"

"How are things going?"

"I'm so proud of you for fighting."

"I just want you to be happy."

"I believe in you."

In many instances, I see my clients receive messaging like this multiple times a day from the people they love while battling their eating disorder. They feel seen, cared for, thought of, helped, and loved in ways they may never have felt before. That connection they've been craving but couldn't name is ever-present and often unrelenting. Clients may push away their family members, their friends, their loved ones, yet people keep fighting for them. It's a noticeable difference from "normalcy" in life.

In reality, it's not feasible for loved ones to engage in this constant communication and expression of worry throughout daily life under normal circumstances. The problem? When clients go from the phase of knowing that many, or even every, person in their life is actively thinking of them, concerned for them, and willing to help them, to "normalcy," they often feel forgotten or less important once they are well. I cannot tell you how many times I've heard, "My family doesn't care anymore," "I'm only loved when I'm sick," "No one pays attention to me unless I'm struggling." A key acknowledgement here is this: They're not *entirely* wrong that there is quite a difference in the dynamics of relationships when struggling vs. not, or not so obviously.

Yes, in *most* instances I see, the family and friends absolutely still love them just as much when they are well as they did when they were more ill. No, they do not show it in the same manner. This is a reality we must accept, and we must remember that not all love felt for someone may be immediately apparent. Unfortunately, the one struggling experiences this "intently obvious" display when sick, so the "less obvious" may feel an extreme of nonexistence. On the other hand, demeanor from loved ones may not always seem to change at all during the course of the disorder. This might leave the individual feeling unloved when they feel others "should be" worried about them, but are not showing it.

Now, in some cases, clinicians and loved ones alike may need to face the fact that love and care may fluctuate with differences in wellness. What I mean by this is as such: Some individuals may really only ever talk with or hear from loved ones when they're seeking treatment, being admitted, struggling with health, or approaching catastrophic outcomes. It is entirely harmful for supportive providers in these individuals' lives to state "They still care, just as much!" when the reality may be that they do not. We must acknowledge that loved ones have their own struggles, their own battles, and their own emotions about their loved one's situation, too. Some families may have created boundaries intentionally to step away from their loved one until they fight for themselves, may "refuse to watch" their loved one harm themselves in this way, or may, unfortunately, have given up on their loved one. Even with this presentation, typically speaking, the loved one didn't remove their love entirely; They simply protected it.

The bottom line of this section, highlighting the worry feeling like love is this: People with EDs are often craving connection, even when they can't admit it. If you are a loved one, use the best of your ability to foster connectedness with the individual at all phases of the process, not just the "scary" part. If you are the one struggling with this notion, please don't let your ED take this and run with it to either get you back or keep you stuck. I see you. I hear you, and I still hope you fight. Love is such a wonderful experience to have in this world: Don't let an ED weaponize it.

Anosognosia

Oh, anosognosia. A fancy term for describing the reality that individuals with eating disorders often have an inability to see their illness. Whether this is seeing the **severity** of or the **presence** of the disorder at all, anosognosia is the culprit as to how individuals are unable to see the reality that others see. Yes, body dysmorphia plays a role here as well, but the overarching symptom that tries to be functional in the presence of the disorder is this anosognosia piece. After all, *why would people fight if they don't realize they are sick?*

This presentation seems to be the hardest for loved ones and for those who don't or haven't struggled. "How do they not see how sick they are?" "Don't they see what they look like?" "Why would they do this to themselves?"

Answer: No, they don't see how sick they are. No, they don't know what they look like. They think "what they're doing to themselves" is what they need to do either to survive, to get through their day, or to even "better" themselves. Yes, they may think what they're doing is harmless.

Anosognosia shows up in many different ways. The one struggling may:

1. Be completely unaware of their disordered ways, and genuinely believe they are functioning well.
2. Have some insight into their rigidity or changed intention on/around food, but believe it's well-intentioned.
3. Have insight that they are functioning in a disordered manner, but believe they have it under control.
4. Acknowledge they're truly struggling with an ED, but lack insight into the severity.
5. See that they are struggling immensely, but believe they won't have bad outcomes.
6. Know they are struggling to a significant degree, but believe they "could still get sicker."
7. Objectively know they must be very ill due to hospital stays and medical concerns, but don't see how close to fatality they may be.

The key idea here is that perception and reality are distorted, significantly affecting both the individual's insight into their disorder and their motivation for recovery. So, what are the outcomes of these presentations?

Example #1. *The one struggling may be utterly unaware of their disordered ways and truly believe they are functioning well.*

More often than not, the initial phases of an eating disorder often aren't "caught" or noticed with concern as the one struggling either normalizes the changes or does not notice them, typically alongside those in their life. Why does the ED love this? Because the individual progresses further into their eating disorder before gaining awareness that anything is wrong. <u>Who would fight back to get better from something they don't even know they have?</u>

Example #2. *The one struggling may have some insight into their rigidity or changed intention on/around food, but believe it's well-intentioned.*

This one really is rooted in societal beliefs. Diet culture **loves** for individuals to focus on their food intake or movement levels, and, more specifically, loves for folks to *strive to improve* in these areas. So, when someone starts to realize they're changing their behaviors around food and exercise, they feel like they're doing something great! Honestly, it may start "great," but an ED may run with the actual positive changes and turn them into a disordered mechanism or motive. This is one of the sneakiest tricks of the ED: to take something that had true positive intentions and affiliations and turn it into a nightmare.

Other people in the individual's life may provide words of praise or encouragement over their "dedication" or "willpower." Doctors may encourage the change, and use language like "keep doing what you're doing!" The individual may temporarily feel better, accomplished, or even "healthful." <u>Who's going to fight back on something **_so great_**</u>?

Example #3. *The one struggling may have insight that they are functioning in a disordered manner, but believe they have it under control.*

I see this often with athletes, but in the general population as well. Someone may be aware that they have crossed into the disordered eating category, but either truly believe they are still *deciding* to do what they are doing, or write it off as "just a part of my sport." Let's also acknowledge that athletes and the general population alike are **surrounded** by disordered eating behaviors. *"It can't be that bad if so many people are doing it, right?"* At this stage specifically, I typically see some insight into the fact that this is not a regular eating pattern or behavior, but also hear how the person could "stop whenever they want." <u>Why stop something you have control over?</u>

Example #4. *The one struggling may acknowledge they're truly struggling with an ED, but lack insight into the severity.*

"Why would I need a higher level of care?" It's so incredibly common for a provider to recommend a higher level of care, have the client not understand why, because they're "not that sick," only to meet with a treatment center and, in fact, be recommended a higher level of care upon that evaluation. This particular experience reminds me of the notion of being "sick enough" for specific amounts or kinds of treatment. Once people accept that they have an eating disorder, the willingness to accept the severity may not always come along with it. More so in this instance, even if individuals can accept how sick they are, they might not accept the level of care or take the steps needed at this level of severity to ensure a safe recovery process and an overall positive prognosis. The ED **loves** to convince the human that it's found a home in that everyone else around them is just being dramatic, and that <u>their current plan of care is just fine.</u>

Example #5. *The one struggling may see that they are struggling immensely, but believe they won't have bad outcomes.*

The "Nothing bad is going to happen; My body can handle it" mentality. The ED has to find weapons where it can. If the individual has gained insight into the severity of the struggle, it still has to limit motivation for recovery in some way. Best way to do this? Convince them that *nothing bad will happen*. A significant issue here is <u>how much</u> individuals struggling "get away with" prior to medical complications arriving, as well as <u>how long</u> they get away with it. Some individuals may see medical complications quite quickly. Though this is not good health-wise, it can sometimes be a helpful motivator for people to fight, as they have obvious signs that their body is struggling. For individuals whose bodies accommodate, adjust, and seemingly "tough it out," this can unfortunately send the signal to the one struggling that their body is "fine" or not in harm's way.

This can be a challenging dynamic, as there are competing beliefs relating to wellness while struggling. On the one hand, the individual may honestly want their body to stay healthy, if for no other reason than to show their providers and loved ones that they're "okay." At the same time, the individual may have a bit of a yearning for their health to deteriorate. Why? Because then they feel valid. Even if and when medical complications arise, the individual will often maintain the belief that these presentations are not catastrophic or extremely harmful in nature. Those things doctors keep warning me about? That only happens to other people, not to me. *My body will be fine.* If nothing bad will happen, why would I stop?

Example #6. *The one struggling may know they are struggling to a significant degree, but believe they "could still get sicker."*

Also known as the "there are other people who are worse than me" mentality. At this point, concern for health and wellness, and insight into such, is now seen through a comparative lens to others. They may have seen movies or social media posts portraying extreme presentations of illness, and decide that they're "not there yet," showing that they'd be fine to continue to decline. Unfortunately, we have to acknowledge that an ED will *never say* that someone has declined enough that they can stop. Sometimes, I believe this is where providers and loved ones alike lose the trust of the one struggling. If an individual who's struggling verbalizes that there are other people out there who are potentially more ill, the response to this matters. Providers and loved ones seem to jump to dismissal of this feeling, with reactions like:

"No, you are just like them!"

"How can you compare your illness when you can't see it?"

"There's no way you could get any worse than this!"

Unfortunately, the one who reported feeling others were worse may, in fact, be right. Now, someone reading this might have a reaction of "NO! Don't compare severities!" Yes, I agree entirely with disengaging with comparative behaviors and thought patterns. However, sometimes acknowledging the truth can actually do some good. Consider responses like:

"Yes, there may be someone out there who is in a worse medical condition than you are. However, it doesn't mean your body will endure what theirs has, or that theirs will continue to endure it much longer."

"Yes, there may be someone out there that is more medically compromised than you, but there's no guarantee they will have the capacity to recover safely and without long-term consequences."

"Yes, someone may have a worse medical presentation than you, but I wonder if they're saying the same thing you're saying to me now: That someone out there must be worse. Let's remember, it will never tell you that you can't keep going; That you should stop now; That you've done enough."

Sometimes, individuals are going to feel like they're being manipulated if you completely ignore the potential truth behind their statement. They will feel unheard, unseen, and therefore unmotivated to challenge this thought if they feel as though you've dismissed a truth. If you can acknowledge where reality may be present while also engaging with recovery-focused language, we can remember that two things can be true at the same time. This may allow the individual to feel seen for how they think, meaning yes, someone may have increased medical complications than they do, but also with the reminder that this thought is a weapon utilized by the disorder to decrease their decision-making capacity further, and bring them further into the disorder to make it a deeper hole to crawl out of.

Example #7. *The one struggling may objectively know they must be very ill due to hospital stays and medical concerns, but don't see how close to fatality they may be.*

Sadly, it may take an actual near-death experience for someone to fully acknowledge why this disorder is currently the deadliest mental health disorder. Even so, once this moment passes, the individual may quickly forget how temporarily fearful they felt for their life. They may even lose someone they've met through the years to the disorder, and still not see it for themselves. The truth of the matter is, the ED wants the individual not to gain insight until it's too late. *"Their bodies were different. Even if others have passed from similar circumstances, you won't,"* it says.

I genuinely believe the anosognosia component is why these disorders are so deadly. If people can't see their sickness at all, see it with limited insight, believe they have almost magical resilience, or genuinely believe they are well, people don't even know they're in a battle where they'd even need weapons, much less take action to use them.

What to remember: You cannot wait for the anosognosia to lift to fight; It may never show the truth until a truly sustained recovery. Yes, you may have to fight before you genuinely believe in or see what you are fighting for. If those around you are telling you you're in a battle, please believe them.

Relentless Thoughts

Do not underestimate how all-consuming an eating disorder can be. This is the one area that is hard to explain without living it. I've often told people,

"It's all you think about."
"It's the first thing you wake up thinking about and the last thought before sleep."
"It's unavoidable."
"It impacts every aspect of your life."
"It's debilitating and relentless."
"You no longer own your own thoughts."
"It never shuts off."

And though I think the message is conveyed clearly through these sentiments, I don't believe the feeling of pervasiveness is always felt. Even if you cannot feel it, please don't underestimate not only the thoughts but also the constant emotional turmoil that comes with them.

I would've given anything back then, anything, for just a moment of peace. A moment of silence. A moment of not feeling at war with my mind. I would be mid-skill/flip as a gymnast, and I would be noticing how the skin on my stomach was folding as I contorted. I'd try to "suck in" during gymnastics skills because I needed to maintain thinness through every moment of my life, athletics included.

During exams, my brain would be focusing on:
- Not letting other people hear my stomach growl
- Wondering if I had eaten enough to truly focus
- Going over in my mind my plan for food for the day
- Trying to think about the question at hand, but getting distracted by the way my stomach was sitting
- Wondering if people thought I had chin rolls looking down at my paper
- Noticing the size of my wrist holding my pencil
- Feeling regretful over choosing to work out yesterday instead of studying
- Reading the same sentence for the 4th time because my comprehension was lagging

I remember asking a friend, "What do you think about when you're taking an exam?" This individual looked perplexed as she answered, "Um, the material? The exam? What else would I be thinking about?"

This is what I mean when I say the thoughts are relentless. I had quite literally forgotten what it felt like to "just" take a test. I like to share an example around mealtime for those who still struggle to understand the mind of one with the disorder. I do acknowledge everyone's brain is different, and their disorder will be as well. Still, the number of times I've heard someone say, "You just described my life" to this example, to me, illustrates that it has to apply to more than just my own past experience.

While everyone else is at the dinner table, laughing and joking about the day, discussing updates on their life, enjoying their meal and their company, the one struggling may be living a very different life in their mind. Here is an example as such. (If you cannot relate to this and struggle with an eating disorder, it simply means our experiences were different. No experience is more objectively "right" or common than another. All disorders are subjective to the one experiencing them.)

Trail of thought:

Ugh, my mom portioned my rice too big again. Doesn't she know to double-check the scoop? Of course, I can't say anything because then she's going to get mad, and it'll cause an argument about food again. Maybe it'll be fine. I think I have time to work out tomorrow, so that should make up for it. Ugh, wait, I have that big project due the next day, so I'm going to need to do that tomorrow. Okay, maybe I could use a different behavior tonight? No, my sister always notices and tells. Okay, perhaps I could just restrict tomorrow, and that will make up for this. Oh NO, I forgot I have to get lunch with my friend who's visiting tomorrow! I do want to see her, but that's just another guaranteed meal. Hm, maybe my family won't notice if I just don't finish the rice. My dad said something last time, but he seems really distracted talking about work. Oh, shoot, you haven't engaged in the conversation in a while. Answer someone, say something of value. Okay, good; Back to business. Alright, I think I'll be able to get my project done in time to also work out; Let's plan on that. But if I can't, then I'll have to restrict the day the project's due. Ugh, I'm going to feel so bloated in the meantime. My therapist told me a lot of this is just fear and anxiety, but I really think this is real and matters this time. I have to figure this out.

What does the world see? Them, smiling and eating. What do family and friends hear? *"Dinner's great, Mom, thank you."*

How does this make the one struggling feel? Completely unseen; Completely alone.

Good thing we are discussing that next.

I've shown how the eating disorder can consume thoughts in and around sports, school, and family. These times even typically provide the best opportunities for distraction for many. If this is what the one struggling's mind looks like when they're "distracted," please acknowledge what it may sound like when they are not; When they're just trying to be alive, and make it through another day.

If you are the one struggling, I'm so sorry if you can relate to any of the above. It's a specific torture that I wouldn't wish upon anyone. I see you, and I'm rooting for you. If you are a loved one or a professional, please meet the one struggling with compassion and patience. Their brain is very loud, and the overwhelm feels constant. Please ask questions about their specific experience to understand better what their thoughts may sound like; The symptoms you cannot see. Please don't meet them with judgment; They are probably already judging themselves. Please let them know that even if you can't understand, you hear them; You see them, and you're willing to do what it takes to help them.

Feeling Alone

"No one truly gets what I feel. No one understands. I don't get to live the same life other people do."

This description emphasizes some common themes of feeling misunderstood, unseen, and **alone**. Some individuals may feel quite literally alone, like they are the only one in this world trapped in the mind they have. They may not have access to a diagnosis, awareness of others who are struggling in similar ways, or the ability to connect with others in a way that feels meaningful. Some, on the other hand, may acknowledge that others may struggle in similar ways or even *know* someone who does, yet still feel isolated and alone in this world.

We have to remember that though some of this feeling is reality-based, some of it is also a deliberate weapon of the eating disorder. On the reality-based side, we have to acknowledge that the one struggling may in fact be the only one feeling this way in some or most environments. At a big family holiday dinner, with 30 people around the table, they may be the only one secretly dying inside. They may be the only one in their grade or on their sports team who struggles. Their family may truly not see or understand the disorder that is at play. We cannot ignore these realities with statements like, "But you're not alone! There are people out there who get you, and I'm right here!" We have to recognize that even though someone is surrounded by loved ones, it doesn't mean their mind feels connected to and seen by them. The "I'm here for you, right here!" is something, don't get me wrong. However, it does not create *community*, a sense of *belonging*, or a shared *common ground*.

So, where does the ED's intentional weapon come in? The feeling of loneliness, being reality-based or not, the ED's voice sounds something like this:

"I'm going to make you feel alone, isolated, and unnoticed by those around you. They don't see you. They'll never see you. And, you'll never get better. Get used to this lonely life, because it's all that you'll ever have."

I'm aware that this language sounds harsh; haunting, even. You are not wrong. I remember writing about my eating disorder for the very first time. Do you want to know the feedback I received?

"The language seems really intense and abrasive, I'd try a different tone."
"That's way too harsh; No one will want to read that."

"That's going to make people sad or feel uncomfortable."
"Consider softening your language."

I'm so glad I didn't.

I refuse to soften my language when discussing the reality that is having an eating disorder, because the ED does not soften its language for anything. I *want* readers to get a glimpse of the feelings of those struggling. I *want* readers who can relate to feel less alone, if even for a moment. The ED is going to tell people they're alone when they really are isolated, to really emphasize their isolation in the world. The ED is going to say to people they're alone when people are all around them, because it will try to convince the one struggling that "they'll never get you." If the ED can convince the one struggling that those around them will never get it or never understand, they might start to lose hope. We learned earlier how important the aspect of hope is in this process. The ED will tell someone that's in a group therapy session, surrounded by others with similar experiences, "But you, you are different. They don't get you. They think they do, but they don't. Even here, you are different."

What I want to illustrate here is this: The ED uses weapons that are highly unrelated to the reality that is present. Don't get too caught up in the logistics of, "but they're so close to their family!" Let's recall from the previous section how constant these thoughts are. If one is hearing lonely language and messaging the majority of their day, though that hour spent with their friend is great, it doesn't often hold a candle to the majority of their life experience.

In addition to these already harmful presentations, the ED then encourages the individual to, in fact, be alone. It will tell the human it's found home in to skip that dinner with their friends, with some excuse of:

o   Needing to lose weight before seeing people
o   Not "needing the extra calories" that dinner may bring
o   Their friends noticing their body's changes
o   Their friends not wanting them there anyway
    (Acknowledge: EDs say you aren't good enough, unloved)
o   You should work out with these hours instead of eating
o   You're too fatigued to go anyway
o   You no longer experience pleasure from things you used
    to anyway, meaning you "won't even have fun."
    (Acknowledge: Strong association with depressive symptoms)

So, now, the individual not only feels alone, but they're quietly literally "choosing" to be alone. Why is this problematic? *Because now the one struggling feels like this experience is their fault.* Somehow, and in some way, the ED always finds a way to shift blame from itself to the one trying to fight or trying to survive. Making them feel alone isn't enough; It has to make them feel like it's their fault, too.

A standard, or simple experience, like going to a mall, can make the one struggling look around and go, "Wow, no one in here has any clue I battle my mind every day." They will look at individuals in the food court and ponder their ability just to eat freely. They may look at clothing stores and see clothing that their ED doesn't let them wear and think, "How do other people feel okay in their body in that?" They may take the stairs to the next floor to burn extra calories and look at those on the escalator, wondering, "Why am I the only one that has to do this? Why isn't their body punishing them for not walking when they have the chance?"

On the other hand, they may take the escalator due to feeling fatigued and look at those on the stairs, wondering what it feels like to feel nourished and energized, and not constantly wondering when their body may fail them, when they may have taken it too far. They'll enter a store, and a worker will say to them, "Welcome in. How are you doing today?" And the one struggling will answer, "Good! How are you?" The worker may answer something like, "Good as well. Let me know if you need anything." This may lead to thoughts of, "Was their answer real or fake like mine? Why would they ask such a stupid question? No, I'm not good. I'm alone. I'm tired. I'm anxious. I'm sad. But I can't tell anyone that, so I try to show them with my body. Clearly, that didn't work either. There's no way to be seen in this world." The person behind them may have had the same interaction and cordially answered to be polite, without the turmoil to follow. I admit there are many more things in this life that could lead to a similar thought pattern, but it's certainly one that can't be ignored in the population struggling with eating disorders.

What do we do with this information? We intentionally show up, day after day, for the one who's struggling. We have lots of thoughts to compete against; We unrelentingly show up for the one with the disorder. We make our presence known. We check in on them more than what may feel natural. We ask them, "What makes you feel most connected when we're together?" We accept the fact that we cannot relate to their exact, uniquely personal experience. We name the fact that this must feel so isolating, and validate how debilitating that must feel. We identify that our own thoughts may not compel us to reach out as frequently as possible, as our own brains are not consumed by this as theirs are. We set alarms. We set reminders. We do the very best we can, but we don't pretend it's enough to fight the voice in their head. We simply ensure to do our part to the very best of our ability.

To the one struggling, I know this book can't combat the language you've heard day in and day out. But, I do hope it can make you feel like someone struggled *similarly,* maybe not the same, but made it out. I hope you feel that even though I am not there, and cannot feel what you're feeling, I care about your story. I believe in your ability to feel connected again in this world. Take the step. Go to the dinner when your mind is screaming at you not to. Call the friend even when the ED says that makes you a "burden." Believe in your ability to find connection again.

Addictiveness

"What would be addicting about something causing so much pain? Unfortunately, so much of it. We have to remember that eating disorders are highly functional disorders. They serve a purpose, even the ones that are unseen. They influence and are influenced by reward pathways. And, wow, are they convincing.

The mechanism that can be observed by those who experience weight loss with their disorder is the component of watching the scale go down. Unfortunately, it can cause magnificent feelings and joyous emotions to watch that number on the scale decrease, day by day, week by week, or month by month. "How low can I go? I want to keep having this feeling. I can't let it stop." Why would the one struggling want to stop their weight loss when it feels so good to see it occur? Those pants that used to be too big that now fall off? The ED *loves* that and temporarily rewards this moment. The problem here is that, like any addiction, you have to *keep using the substance to get the desired outcome*. It's not enough to just see the scale go down once. To get the feeling again, the number must go down again. I think it's obvious why this cycle becomes so dangerous. (Acknowledge: This experience is not relatable to all eating disorders, only when the symptom of weight loss is present and desired.)

Again, a mechanism observed for those experiencing weight loss as a symptom of their disorder is the amount of compliments and comments one may receive. "You look so great! Did you lose some weight? Wow, I wish I had your willpower! Your body looks amazing; You're like a model!" These affirmations can feel **so** nice for the brain, which is typically being beaten up each day. *Why gain the weight back and lose all of this affirmation and confidence?*
(Acknowledge: This experience is not relatable to all eating disorders, only when the symptom of weight loss is present and desired.)

Unfortunately, eating disorder behaviors themselves can also be quite addictive. We can look at them one by one for a few examples of this.

If we look at the behavior of restriction, it is not unfamiliar with compulsive and pleasure-seeking principles. One example may be when an individual sets a goal (really, their ED does) and achieves it. This may look like, "I'm going to restrict dinner tonight." If the individual accomplishes this, the ED gives a reward and says, "Great work! You did awesome! If you do it again, I'll let you feel happy again then, too!" Wow, what a relief and a break from the constant yelling, which the one struggling is used to hearing. How compelling to do it again... So, the individual does it again: Sets a goal like restricting dinner again tomorrow. And, what do you know, the ED celebrates the individual **again!** It engages with messaging like, "Great work! I'm so proud of you. You are so strong and determined. I'll reward you with happy feelings again for listening."

If we look at the behavior of purging, the correlation to addiction is most closely associated with the immediate, instant, if you will, gratification. That ED has been screaming at them and yelling at them for how much they ate. It's shaming them, degrading them, and not letting them forget its disappointment in them for eating what they did. But then, the individual engages with purging. Immediately, the ED says, "Well done. You've solved this problem today. I'm proud of you. Now, remember this lesson tomorrow." The individual gets met with sighs of relief and, maybe, something resembling silence when they use this behavior. It's amazing what people will do for some peace and quiet in their minds when it's so hard to find. A week or so later, the ED is yelling at the individual again, berating them for the dinner they just had. Immediately, the brain goes, "I know what will make us feel better." So, the individual purges again. The ED again congratulates and says they've done something good, and eases their mind for a moment from the usual torment it prescribes.

(Acknowledge: Similarity to exercise presentation here.)

Bingeing, though *followed up by* emotions of shame or guilt, in the moment can feel freeing. All of that stress and chaos from the day? Gone- "I'll let you just dive into the food and forget about the rest of your problems for the moment. I'll let you get so many bites repetitively of utter and sheer enjoyment and flavor; I'll pacify your day." Granted, insight following this behavior often leaves the individual saying, "That was the last time; I won't do that again. It doesn't last." However, the ED tries again later. "Are you feeling overwhelmed?" It asks. "I have a solution for you..." It taunts. The individual engages again, giving their worries to their pantry, and stuffing down their pain. It works, but only for a moment.

You might ask now, "So what's the problem? It works!" The problem lies in both the consequences and the progression. Any severity of engaging with an eating disorder behavior is going to carry potential consequences: Some emotional, some physical. However, the mechanism I'd like to emphasize is that of progression being the problem. That celebration it used to give when they'd succeed with the number going down? It no longer provides. It shifts from "Well done! You did so great!" to

"I expect more from you. This isn't enough yet. Keep going, though, and I'll celebrate you then."

When restricting the meal used to lead to language of "Awesome job. You are so strong and resilient and tough!" It now only meets the individual with this once they've upped the severity. "Restricting dinner is no longer going to impress me. Restrict for a longer period of time if you want me to be proud of you." So, the individual may follow the demand and, in fact, restrict longer. Initially, messaging may be celebratory, but they again won't last. "Go longer," it will say. "I'll celebrate you once you truly impress me with how much you limit. Today was not good enough."

When purging the food used to bring a sense of accomplishment and joy, it now just brings mild relief. "You shouldn't have eaten so much in the first place," it says. That binge that used to alleviate the burdens of the day successfully, temporarily, now also carries burdens of its own.

So, *why don't they just stop then?*
Because it's not that simple.

If you think about any addiction, you can agree that often, not always, the individual has insight into the damage being done, and that they're no longer receiving the positive feelings they may have been at the beginning of the addiction. So, why don't they stop? Because the addiction has taken over their mind. It's isolated them, removed them from their values, taken away opportunities, and consumed their life. The thing that used to bring them joy now only allows them to feel as though they can survive. Who's going to give that up?

This is the part of the process that is so hard. You are going to feel worse before you feel better. The scale example that went from getting celebrated when the number went down, to getting mild relief when the number went down, to still getting yelled at when the number went down: That ED probably is not going to be very polite or palatable when that number starts going up, whether you "see it" or not. The restriction example is the same: The celebration, relief, yelling... That ED is going to *really* try to punish you when the restriction is omitted. The thoughts will not be stopped following mealtime when purging is removed from the table, leading to more unrelenting nights in the ED, making sure you know you're not listening to what it says. Therefore, it won't give you peace. The anxiety transfers to other eating habits when trying to cease the bingeing, inciting fear over typically enjoyed meals.

The good news is: There is an end. The urges will subside over time. They don't subside as quickly as I wish they could... but they do dissipate. It's getting there, that is the challenge. It's trusting that the discomfort won't last forever. It's believing that the way out is not only worth it, but possible. It's taking the leap of faith knowing that discomfort will temporarily follow. It's getting ready for the fight of your life. Recovery is possible. Yes, even for you. The ED will throw everything at you to make you return to your substance of choice: Don't let it convince you it will bring you lasting joy when only true <u>freedom</u> can bring you that.

Competition

A way I like to describe this phenomenon is,

You're competing, but you can't see what you're competing with accurately. The people in your life don't know you're competing against them; The mirror certainly does. You're competing against the people you only see through a screen, too.

That trophy you hope to win? You can't even climb the podium to receive it, much less have the energy to hold it high.

This might be one of my favorite symptoms to discuss, simply because it's one that carries so much shame for the one struggling. I hope talking about it can destigmatize this for even just one person.

The eating disorder tells you that you need to be the sickest. It tells you to look around, and ensure you are the thinnest; Ensure you are using the behaviors to the utmost of your possible severity. It forgets to tell you that you don't have access or insight to see your severity to know what you're competing with, but tells you you're in the arena, nonetheless.

Looking back, it's so interesting to me the people I competed against. I competed against people who (seemingly) had wonderful relationships with food. I competed against those who more apparently did not have good relationships with food. I competed with those who were in similar body types to mine. I competed with those who were thinner than I was. I competed with those who ate less than I did. I'm not sure when, but my life turned into an arena, and it was go-time.

It's not because I needed something to compete in; I already was a great student, challenging myself to excel compared to my peers. I was also a D1 athlete, always striving to be the best I could be. More so, striving to be perfect. I was a gymnast, of course. Perfection was the goal. So, why compete with my body and my intake, too? *Because eating disorders impact everyone, obvious competitor or not.*

Let's talk about how this competition shows up. It may show up at the dinner table with family. The one struggling may try to eat the slowest, eat the least, or show the least enjoyment. It may show up at practice, when someone wants to order the smallest size uniform on the team, or have the thinnest (insert body part of hyperfocus here). It might show up in the classroom, wanting to be the thinnest individual in the room. Maybe it shows up on Thanksgiving, being the one to practice and illustrate the "most control."

I want to give special attention to treatment settings here. During my time in treatment, I remember feeling different. *Not sick enough,* even. It seemed as though every patient compared themselves to others, as if there were an unspoken hierarchy of who had achieved the most with this disorder. "I've been admitted x number of times, I've had this health consequence x number of times." It's as if losing more of your life meant you were winning in treatment. How long you stayed in treatment seemed to matter. I remember being so confused why someone would be sad to step up from Residential to PHP (Partial Hospitalization Program), until I understood it for myself. It's as if so many factors influenced validity, and most of them were unspoken.

- How thin you were
- How much weight you lost
- Your BMI
- The amount of concern your treatment team had for you
- Your level of care
- How long you stayed at each level of care
- How many times you went to each level of care
- If you were "resistant" enough
- If you cried
- If you supplemented vs completed
- If you relapsed
- How many times you relapsed

o   How long you had been sick

o   How often you engaged with your behaviors

o   If you had medical complications associated with your illness

o   How bad those medical complications were

o   What your mood was like around meal time

o   How you reported you felt after you ate

o   How quickly you made progress

This is the part that I think a lot of folks without eating disorders miss. That, no, this is not fake, fabricated, or made up. However, some behaviors or symptoms may present as a function of the disorder's competitiveness, leading to a sense of validity rather than the reasons the client shares verbally or others may assume. There's this list of rules one is supposed to follow, ways to act, what to say, and how to struggle. The ED tells you to compete in all aspects, as listed above. The more boxes you check off? Well, the ED rewards you for checking off each one. An example of an individual acting in a manner in which to compete rather than what is genuine is as follows:

It took me *so* long to admit that I, someone diagnosed with an eating disorder, would sometimes look forward to meals in treatment. To those reading this who struggle with an ED, you know that the ED tells you to **never** admit to this, to **only** portray the struggles and the challenges. Before some meals, I'd quite literally be hungry, maybe even wanting food. Yes, these were complex feelings, often accompanied by fear; however, the desire was there nonetheless.

However, how would I verbally check in before and after the meal?

Pre-meal: "I'm very anxious about this meal and still full from the last meal." (was actually hungry and kind of wanting food)

Post-meal: "I'm really overfull and anxious from eating that when I didn't want to." (Was probably pretty full and anxious, but not to the degree I reported; Might've, in fact, wanted to eat the food.)

After all, that's what we all were saying.

Don't get me wrong. There were meals that were hard. Meals I dreaded. Meals I felt so uncomfortably full after. Meals I carried so much guilt and regret over eating. However, the other times existed too, and I thought I wouldn't be taken seriously if I admitted to them. Years later, I finally asked someone, "Did you... ever... um... look forward to meals in treatment?" I was astonished when they said yes. Then, I asked another friend the same thing. They provided the same answer of something along the lines of, "Yes, I sometimes would, but I never told anyone." As you can imagine, I got many more yeses over the years, which is why I'm bringing it to any reader's attention here.

What? Why didn't we just admit this? Why didn't we say we were hungry? Why didn't we say that our fear was coupled with enjoyment? *Why were we so ashamed of our true experience?*

Let's also make note that the professionals seemed to take you more seriously this way. We also cannot ignore the media portrayal of these disorders, basically showing the one struggling "how they're supposed to act." Much of the disorder was real. Many meals were horrifying. And, the ones that weren't were not admitted to. Looking back, I wish someone had asked me about this dynamic sooner. I'm not sure if I would've been honest, but it would've intrigued me about the *why* behind their question.

If you are reading this, and you've ever secretly looked forward to a meal but pretended you didn't, it's okay. It doesn't take away your validity. You're in good company. If you are reading this as a loved one or a professional, please hear the actual message I'm trying to convey. The one struggling is still very ill, whether they fear every meal or not. If we can accept that two things can be true at once, meaning the individual struggles at some times and does better in others, and *still is quite sick*, we open the door to more honest discussion about what's driving the behaviors, leading to more authentic cognitive progress.

If you are reading this and you *haven't* had the experience of secretly looking forward to or liking a meal, you are just as valid as anyone else. I continue to hold out hope and belief in you that you can look forward to food again someday, enjoy it, and even admit it. I'm sending you, too, strength and support from afar at this time. Whatever your emotions are towards food, and I know it can change by the minute, you are valid in your experience.

Lying

Behavioral, habitual, compulsive, and intentional: The ways in which lying presents within an eating disorder. No one likes to be lied to. With this, I agree entirely. And also, I want to share a few reasons as to why we hold compassion and patience for those with eating disorders who are struggling with the truth.

- The lies are often functional (serving a purpose)
- Avoiding the truth allows one to create one's own reality, maybe a more comfortable or *controlled* one, if you will.
- They may be fearful of consequences, showing insight into that the decisions they are making may have bad outcomes.
- They might believe the lies themselves, as a way to get through such a torturous disorder.
- They may not realize they are doing it at all.
- The lies may have become addictive, almost like a challenge to see how long the act can be kept up.
- They might feel ashamed of their truth.
- They might struggle with distinguishing reality from not at the moment.

o   If what they eat is no longer in their control, *what they say* to people may be all that they have left that's theirs and theirs only.

So, why is it so hard to maintain patience with someone struggling when they lie to you? This is because it often disrupts us at our core, or our values, and the respect we carry for ourselves and expect from others. What do we do with this information? We remember that this situation <u>is not about us.</u> The one suffering is not spending extra energy and time thinking, "Wow, lying to them will be very disrespectful to their psyche and probably upset their value system." Let's remember, the energy that they have, they are often simply using to survive. Unfortunately, surviving may feel like lying some days.

Now, don't get me wrong, this behavior still needs to be corrected. These functional components must be worked through to translate into new, adaptive mechanisms. And also, this will take time. Try to view the lying as a symptom of the disorder, which it is. Yes, the expression of this symptom has the capacity to impact others, but it is a symptom nonetheless. It's also one of the more visible ones, meaning it tends to become a pillar people tend to focus on often.

So, how to stop lying? I generally recommend a midday and evening check-in on communications thus far throughout the day. At around halfway through the day and before winding down for bed, I recommend that individuals take 5 minutes and reflect on the words they've said this day, and how they've portrayed their recovery or struggles to others verbally. If someone doesn't have much interaction in their schedule, this check-in might need to be amended. "Based on my behavior engagement so far today, would I share about them honestly if someone asked?" If someone did have more opportunities for expression of progress, then they assess for the validity of communication, and the why behind it.

Maybe their mom asked them if they were going to eat breakfast, and they said they would on their way to school, but didn't. At the half-day check-in, this provides the individual the opportunity to correct the behavior and even correct the communication. This individual may not have had seemingly any intention to lie to their mom, as it may have been "habit" to answer in this way, harm avoidance in case mom would get mad if the individual said no, neutral if the individual did not think further about the interaction, or protective if the ED said they weren't supposed to have breakfast that day (protective from the ED wrath, that is).

What can they do now? Depending on where they're at in the recovery process, I'd have hopes that the client could, in fact, follow the recommendations from their Dietitian on what to do when they skip a meal: engage in a recovery-focused action and consider sharing the situation with mom to shed light on the truth and reality. Yes, this is easier said than done due to the reasoning discussed above. This brings me to the point that we should not be looking at all lies the same way. It's very easy to count how many times a client lies in a day, a week, or a month. It also doesn't give us much information. Instead, I'd recommend keeping track of the "Lie Whys." The why behind the lie often gives us much more useful information in itself, rather than just the fact that it happened.

For example, an individual may have reported lying about food 15 times this month. Yes, this is helpful information regarding the pathology of their disorder, as well as for assessing progress in treatment. And, it didn't give us very much useful information as to how to move forward or cease this behavior. Instead, I'd recommend keeping track of the truths vs lies, but not writing down a lie without the why behind it. Here's a visual difference on how this can be helpful therapeutically.

Lying Chart: *Underline days you lied about your intake.*

Monday	Tuesday	Wednesday	Thursday	Friday	Saturday	Sunday

Insights gained: The individual was not forthcoming about intake for 4 days this week.

Lies and Whys Chart: *Underline days you lied about your intake. Below, write why you felt compelled to lie in this moment.*

Monday	Tuesday	Wednesday	Thursday	Friday	Saturday	Sunday

Tuesday: *My mom always over-portions my snack. I really did want to eat a snack, but I didn't trust her not to grossly over-portion it, even though my dietitian has consistently told her not to. So, I lied and said I had already eaten when I hadn't really. I just couldn't trust what she'd put on my plate.*

Wednesday: *I really did intend to eat my afternoon snack, but then some friends from school invited me to play ball with them in the park, and I just really wanted to go have fun. I told my mom I had already eaten so that she'd let me go. Otherwise, I think she would've made me be late since she doesn't like me eating right before movement without time to "digest."*

Friday: *Today, I was just really fatigued with recovery. I wasn't hungry and just didn't want to force myself at school for once. I*

just felt like I needed a break, but I knew my mom would get
mad if I said that, as she'd say I "didn't take it seriously."

Saturday: *I really just forgot. Completely, I forgot. My friends*
and I got caught up at the beach; I didn't even realize I hadn't
eaten the snack I packed. I knew I couldn't tell my mom it was
an honest mistake because she wouldn't believe me.

Insights gained: The Individual wasn't forthcoming about intake
4 times this week—trust concerns identified between the
individual and mom. Need for discussion around "real life"
activities and how to ensure intake is still met while not missing
out on being present and spontaneous. Work through treatment
fatigue reporting and ways to combat urges associated.

Do we see the difference in assessment/outcome? Remember:
It's crucial to discuss the outcomes of this activity with
compassion and a motivation for improvement, not in a punitive
tone. Punishment for honest engagement with this activity
increases the likelihood of future dishonesty.

Now that we've identified that lying is common within
the presentation of these disorders, it's time also to
acknowledge that not everyone with an eating disorder will lie,
and distinguishing between reporting the truth or a lie can be a

challenge for a loved one or a professional alike. People cannot lose sight of the fact that individuals with eating disorders are often mistrusted, sometimes not for reasons congruent with their behaviors. A saying I use to describe this phenomenon is,

In a Court of Law, you are considered innocent until proven guilty. When you have an eating disorder, you're often considered guilty until proven innocent.

I like to use this example because it demonstrates the difference between life before and after diagnosis. Of course, the differences are immense, but the assumptions from others that shift cannot be ignored. Now, being inquisitive and curious about an individual with an eating disorder's reporting is entirely justified, due to the possibility of dishonesty. We need to remember to keep our framework there, as inquisitive and curious rather than accusatory.

For example, if someone who is struggling says they can't make it to dinner because they've already made plans to eat with their partner, it's okay to be curious about the honesty of their reporting. We acknowledge that the words may not always be of face value. And also, accusing someone of lying when they are in fact eating dinner with their partner will rupture trust, lessen rapport, enhance a divide, and overall create chaos that is not motivating nor helpful for the individual. If you accuse and are right, the odds of them responding, "You're right! Thanks for catching me. I did lie about dinner tonight. I'll make sure to go to your dinner now," are incredibly low. They're more likely to defend the lie, heighten emotion, deepen a divide, and, overall, create chaos that is neither motivating nor helpful. Sound familiar?

This shows the amount of nuance, intention, and compassion that needs to be given to addressing these sorts of issues. Instead of "I know you don't actually already have a dinner planned and you wanted an excuse to get out of eating," try "Okay, no worries on the dinner. You will be missed. I hope all is well, and please let me know if, for some reason, going to a dinner right now is a trigger or challenge I'm unaware of. I know you have dinner with your partner, but I want you to know I'm willing to listen if your struggles ever impact your ability to engage with our plans. Proud of you for fighting!" This response doesn't directly question the validity of the friend's reasoning for not attending the dinner, but it does open up the dialogue of discussing the possibility that this dinner could have been a challenge. It welcomes discussion and makes one feel safe to respond appropriately.

For the one curious about "if they're lying or not," I will say that this is an excellent moment of joining in the individual's fears. You, too, are not in control of something! You, too, cannot guarantee a reason or outcome and its validity. This is what the one struggling faces each day: feeling utterly and tirelessly not in control. That unknown, uncomfortable feeling you get when you can't be sure about their answer? That's what they face when they challenge their behaviors: unknown and uncomfortable emotions.

Granted, there are going to be presentations where the eating disorder is quite obviously lying. In these instances, I encourage the individual and their treatment team to outright discuss the topic of transparency and honesty in sessions, and ways to work through these challenging moments. Sometimes, if I have an inkling that my client may be struggling with the truth about something, I'll reflect:

"You do not have to tell me what it is. I'm getting the sense that there's something you're not comfortable with telling me yet. Is there something you have not been able to be honest about just yet? You don't have to share anything more than a yes or no."

You'd be amazed at how many times you'll hear a, "I'm not ready to discuss it yet, but yes, there is something." There, we actually just made a step forward. We admitted what we've reported is not congruent with reality, and we also accepted that we aren't ready to face it head-on yet. That's okay. This honesty was still a great practice, showing the psyche that the individual can report things consistent with their real experience, and they had just taken the first step in doing so.

"Why be honest if I'm not going to be believed anyway?", another perspective we need to be aware of. An ED can weaponize this to justify using a behavior, since people will "assume they did anyway." Yes, maybe an individual has lied about using a behavior in the past. And, also, they might not be lying this time. We have to give them room to grow, change, and progress without questioning every step of the way. We also need to ensure that if we do have doubts about someone's behavior or truthfulness, it's truly because of their behavior alone, and not due to any personal fears about their disorder. EDs impact those around them in many ways; One of which is their own fear of the unknown. Meaning, worries of loved ones or professionals can manifest as mistrust, further leaving the individual feeling alone or misunderstood.

If it truly seems as though an individual may be struggling with the truth of what they're reporting, I recommend approaching them to discuss it rather than *accusing them*. Acknowledge that in this moment, the truth may still be hard for them. Everything within them is screaming to protect their lie. The battle in their mind may temporarily override the true self, trying to discuss. Yes, validity is important; Remembering that they are human first, not just a walking eating disorder, is even more important. Give credit and grace where you can, while modeling your engagement with language that mirrors reality for them. This will do more than you know.

Secrecy

"Why didn't they tell me?" is a question I'm far too familiar with in this line of work. The answer? ***Pick your reason.*** To understand why this question is asked is to understand the pathology of an eating disorder. A few reasons that come to mind immediately and seem to present the most often are…

The individual:

- Does not see their sickness themselves (telling someone is not even considered because, *tell them what?*
- Thinks they're doing something well, being healthy even. The people around them are commenting positively on the changes. They see the new behaviors already. So, *tell them what?*
- Has been telling those around them about their newfound focus on food/body, just using language not inclusive of an eating disorder, but rather of normalcy. Again, *tell them what?*
- Is protecting their eating disorder. After all, if they tell others about their actual, disordered experience, *they may try to take it away.*

- o Is ashamed by their eating disorder. *Why would I tell them something I'm so ashamed of?*
- o Is fearful they won't be understood, or may even not be believed. *"If I don't take my experience seriously, why would other people?"*
- o Are simply, listening to what their ED says to and not to do. We can all take a good guess at what the ED's language is to the individual about telling other people: **Don't.**

So often here, loved ones or professionals in the individual's life have their own sadness, frustration, anger, or confusion when the revelation of the ED occurs.

"How could I miss this?"

"Did they not trust me?"

"Was I not welcoming enough?"

"What did I do to make them hide this from me?"

"I thought we had a better relationship/rapport than this."

All of these thoughts above? Completely valid. And also highly related to those trying to help the individual who's struggling, rather than the individual's presentation itself. Loosely put, those in the life want to "figure out" why the individual didn't confide in them. The straightforward answer might be: *This isn't about you.* This disorder may be the most personal struggle the individual has ever lived through. Meaning, whether someone was "welcoming" or not, or whether they showed active care, the individual's decision to come forward with their personal information is separate from the reality at hand. Maybe people in their lives weren't welcoming or comforting, and didn't create an environment that fostered honesty and vulnerability. The ED still most likely used this to its advantage. This needs to be worked through, but maybe with some time. Attention should be given to the one struggling's emotions first, as subduing them most likely contributed to this presentation in the first place.

Have you ever lived under a microscope? A question we must remember when trying to understand how an individual's life may change once their ED is out in the open. People begin monitoring meals, asking questions about intake, questioning bathroom trips, and assessing for behavior change. A disorder that values perceived control certainly hates this. The other problem with being under a microscope is seeing things that maybe weren't intended to be seen. What do I mean by this? Say a young kiddo loves butterflies. They love the colors and the way they fly, and how beautiful they look to the naked eye. What can happen if the kiddo sees that beautiful butterfly under a microscope, and sees some beady eyes or hairy legs? The butterfly can no longer choose how it wants to be seen by the world, putting their vulnerabilities on display. I'm not sure if the kiddo finds the butterfly to be quite so enchanting anymore. Granted, some of this needs to be worked through in therapy. This overt attention to what someone shows the world can absolutely be pathological in nature. And, also, it can just be human. What are some things that you hide from the world yourself? How would it feel if people had access to them? This can maybe explain further why the one struggling's mood can shift so much: Worst fears become exposed. The moral of the story here is as follows: Yes, looking more closely can be incredibly helpful for identifying the disorder's presentation and, therefore, recovery efforts around it. And the microscope may reveal things that didn't need to be seen, leaving the one struggling even more vulnerable than imagined.

To further this analogy, let's also not forget the idea of a magnifying glass burning, or leading to fire. If you look at something under a magnifying glass and angle the sunlight above it, a little flame can be produced. The problem with humans? If you have a specific stimulus angled just at the right spot in someone's life, it may show you some destruction that wasn't there prior to you looking, or was truly self-created. What's an example of this? It's focusing too closely on a detail that you are unsure of whether it is relevant or not, and gleaming some revelation of importance out of it. It's turning the mole hill into a mountain. It's noticing *something* but attributing it to more. It's noticing that a loved one always goes to the bathroom two hours after eating. <u>So, you look closer.</u> Wow, it's really every time! This is so rigid and habitual. What are they hiding? <u>So, you look closer.</u> Their eyes sometimes are pretty red when they leave too- I've really caught them now. <u>So, the light hits the magnifying glass.</u> I realized they're quieter once they return from their bathroom trip. This makes so much sense after hiding something. Yes, this presentation could indicate purging behavior. *Not in this instance, though.*

Why was the loved one going to the restroom 2 hours after meals? To prevent oneself from purging, to ensure not going into a triggering environment too soon after the activating stimulus (the meal). Why every time? Because they're showing up for their recovery efforts every chance they get, not allowing the ED a single opportunity to gain a win. "But what about the eyes?" She sometimes cries when presented with her trigger. She remembers what she's put herself through in the past and recalls the pain she's endured in this environment. "But why so withdrawn upon return?" Because she doesn't get her release anymore. She's choosing to fight instead. Yes, this may take the energy out of her mood.

Secrecy exists in eating disorders due to it being an eating disorder's favorite weapon, but also because of how human behavior around the individual can be expected. Unfortunately, specifically when fear is present, the stimulus from those around the individual, in fact, will have the sun angled the right way to cause chaos where there wasn't any. "Why didn't they just tell me why they go to the bathroom after 2 hours exactly each time? Then I wouldn't have to find my own reasons." Well, my first reflection is... "Did you ask?" Followed up with, "Did you believe the answer?" People don't tend to offer up their secrets without probing. They share them when the opportunity presents and when they feel that someone will respond well to them. Furthermore, people don't tend to say things when they have an inkling they won't be believed. So, if you answered "no" to either question above and chose to utilize your microscope instead, know you might see things that weren't meant to be or don't carry realistic implications for reality.

Let's also remember how food is one of the very few things in this world one can have total control over. Everyone else gets to have a role in other areas of life, *"I just want this one thing to be mine."* Unfortunately, it can feel quite empowering to maintain an entirely personal secret for so long. It can feel like you're in control of your world when other people don't have access to see it accurately. It can make you feel like others can't take everything away from you, as they don't even know there's something of yours to take. It keeps you in good standing with the eating disorder, as it says "good work" for keeping this a secret for another day. Maintaining the secrecy is protective in and of itself. I'll state again, as someone on the outside of the disorder, this presentation is not about you; It's about them, their safety, their choices, their fears, and their autonomy in this world. It's about their life.

So, what's the difference between secrecy and lying? Why put them in separate sections? Well, the demeanor behind these two words holds two very different functions of the disorder. Lying is manipulative, controlling, protective, compulsive, and almost game-like. Almost everyone can agree that lying has a societal connotation of being "bad." Secrecy, on the other hand, can nearly be held in high regard. "Can you keep a secret?" You may ask someone, assessing their character, morals, and strength to keep something within and to themselves. When someone entrusts you with their secret, you feel chosen, flattered, and even special. Well, how do we think the one struggling feels when they successfully keep their own secret within? Strong: they didn't share it with others they couldn't trust. Obedient: as they listened to the disorder's wishes. Powerful: as they've overcome moments where they almost slipped. Special: as they have something that's only theirs. Alive: as it's exciting to keep a secret that, deep down, you know others have an opinion on.

This shows the part of the disorder that many don't seem to see or that they more easily forget about. The ED does, in fact, have the capacity to lead to a **lot** of good emotions or feelings. Does it last? Maybe not. Does it come with repercussions? Most certainly. But the good moments are there nonetheless, and the secrecy protects them.

Objectively, and unfortunately, often realistically, *"People won't get it. Why would I tell them anyway?"*

This highlights the reasoning and need for more widespread knowledge, understanding, and perception of eating disorders. People don't want to tell someone something and then be judged for it; That's a very well-accepted sentence. When people talk, they want to be understood and seen. I do wonder if people felt that society better understood the presentation of these disorders and how they function, whether individuals would be more open to sharing without stigma and assumptions.

Losing Yourself

"I don't even recognize you right now," a sentence many individuals with EDs have heard, referencing a potential visual change, but more so a personality shift. Another popular saying might be, "I don't even know who you are anymore." Well, the one struggling can take this in one of a few ways.

For myself, I acknowledged I had lost the true me at some point. However, I held a belief that some of the eating disorder's values were those of my own. An example that comes to mind is just how much I lost. I didn't know who I wanted to be and how I wanted to live, much less what brought me joy in this world. However, I did know that I could control my weight, considered achieving new goals of the ED as "enjoyment," and thought, *"I'm not sure who I'll be in the future, but I know I want to be thin."* What was hard about this statement was that I really believed this came from my true self. I remember thinking, "I just really value thinness. Why aren't these people getting that?" "These people," referring to providers and loved ones voicing other perspectives, like, "maybe that's your ED talking." I simply wouldn't have it.

As you can see, it's easy to not only lose yourself, but then find yourself through the guise of your eating disorder. I knew I still loved my friends and family, but I was willing to miss time with them to engage with my disorder. I still maintained gratitude for those who had concern, but I chose to fight their wishes instead. It felt like an inability to access who I truly was inside.

On the one hand, the individual may truly not recognize themselves, either physically or emotionally. They might have completely lost their identity, feeling fully consumed by the desires of the disorder. Those things you miss? They miss too. Their laugh, you haven't heard in a while? They don't have the energy for. Their sense of humor? Takes too much brain power and joy. Their academics? Their ED controls their engagement with this. Their relationships? Who has time for that when there's so much to keep track of regarding intake and movement? Their ability to follow through? Every day is different for them now. The things they used to love? The ED ripped away.

The eating disorder can truly find a way to weasel into every part of someone's life. The insight into this will vary. This is why it's so important to honor that yes, the ED exists, but that the individual still exists as well; We just have to find them and nurture them out. Engaging with the language of "missing" an individual due to the presence of an ED may be helpful and reflective, highlighting that others valued the true self better over what the ED provides. However, it may be hindering if the individual has a fear of never getting back to themselves, blaming themselves for the disappointment of those around them. A simple solution to this? Ask the individual how this sort of commentary makes them feel. Talk with them about their perceptions of their identity and their thoughts on this. Know that they too miss being themselves and actively alive in this world. With many people endorsing thinking about food and body the majority of their day in the presence of the ED, remember the role this plays in how much time or brain space is left just to be themselves, and who they used to be. They probably want out, too: We don't always have to remind them they're still stuck. Something tells me <u>they know.</u>

On the flip side, someone may have felt like they lost themselves before the disorder, and that the ED helped them to find themselves. For maybe the first time in their life, they might feel like they know who they are. They know what they do each day. They know their decisions. They know their dynamic in the world. They control how much space they take up, emotionally and physically. They feel confident in their description of themselves as the:

o   Sick one

o   Thin one

o   One who eats very little

○ One who eats a lot

○ One who has "willpower"

○ One who loves the gym

○ One with drive

○ One who doesn't need enjoyment from food as others do

○ One who can say no to things others can't

Is this a well-rounded identity? Maybe not. Is it, in fact, an identity that someone could *feel* strong in? Unfortunately, so. With this presentation, the individual might not miss the old self. They might feel as though the old self's identity wasn't strong, impressive, or unique. Though I truly believe the individual's true self is still in there, it doesn't mean someone wants it back.

The idea of losing yourself is a nuanced one, as maybe someone feels they've maintained who they are throughout their disorder. Though this presentation might be more rare, it's not impossible. If anything, they might feel like they are now an improved version of themselves, with their rigidity crossing over into school, influencing improved grades, determination crossing into their athletics, influencing their work ethic at practice, or their need for approval physically crossing into the emotional, influencing their ability to show up for their friends and family. This segment is a tough one, as these three presentations may even change with time.

If you are the one struggling, acknowledge that any presentation, including one that's not listed here today, is valid and worthy. If you relate to feeling as though you've lost yourself, know that you can find yourself again. Meet them with grace and compassion as they fearfully hide during this time, trying to protect themselves. Meet yourself with the same grace as you look in the mirror, and *know* you'll get the real you back. Don't listen when the ED says the true you is gone forever or incapable of making a return. Take that as a sign of how much the ED wouldn't want that for you. After all, as your true self, you have way too much capacity to fight. Know it doesn't want this. If you relate to feeling like you like yourself more in your disorder, give yourself the same grace and compassion as above. Acknowledge the functional components that have seemingly improved your life, but don't let it overshadow where it's hindered. Maybe your identity is flexible now, and that's okay. You're allowed to reinvent yourself; Don't let the ED reinvent for you.

Whether it's an old you, a new you, or a current you that you're fighting for, try not to get caught up in the prefixes. **Fight for you,** whoever that is. No rule says you must be who you were "before" in order to succeed in recovery. If anything, the topic of success in recovery probably warrants its own book.

Fight for the part of you that believes you deserve good. Fight for the part of you that had passions and goals, even if they were different from others. Fight for the you that is flawed, because they are enough just as they are. You deserve to come back to yourself; You might just feel unsure of who that is in the moment. Have faith that you will know again, and that the relinquishing of the ED can provide this. Fight for yourself, which may look like an unknown list of identity descriptors. **You'd be amazed at what you can do with a blank slate.**

My Story in Writing

I wrote this piece after a few years of sustaining my eating disorder recovery. I hope it can make you feel seen, heard, and understood for the struggle that is having an eating disorder. Everyone's story is unique, and I'm sure you may struggle in ways that I did not. However, I hope this message leaves you feeling less alone and with a new sense of hope that recovery can happen for you, too.

"Save yourself," they said. "Help yourself," they said. " But didn't they know I couldn't?

I'll never forget the day a loved one told me, "I refuse to go to your funeral soon, Maria. I will not do it." I believe that's the moment it hit me- I really could die from this. What was crazy, though? Everyone around me was sobbing. They were crying, hysterical over my deterioration. But myself? I felt nothing. Nothing, had become my new normal.

As someone who's in recovery from their eating disorder, most would expect that I would use only negative or even angry words to describe life during this time. Instead, I think of two very different pictures: one is beautiful and shiny and sunny and magical, and the other is complete darkness. On the sunny side, I would describe my time in anorexia as a form of bliss. I felt confident in my capabilities. I was proud of what I was able to do to my body. I felt powerful being able to take my body beyond its limit. I felt invincible with how I could starve and batter my body, and stay alive. I felt safe knowing I was doing something about my pain. I felt secure shrinking myself into a body that no one would want to abuse or take advantage of. I felt unseen, hiding in the shadows of my own life. I felt beautiful with each new bone that made its appearance. I felt, special.

The other picture, though, is not so pretty. I despised myself. I hated every inch on my skin. I prayed for my organs to shrink. I laid awake sobbing over how my stomach was lying while I rested. My throat was throbbing from nails attempting for just "one more" release. My stomach screamed for attention and hastily woke me up each night. My insides hurt from the combinations of behaviors used. My joints begged me to stop, while I upped the incline on the treadmill. My skin burned from the ice I placed on my chest while my heart was struggling to beat. I woke up, sad to see another day every morning. Another day at war with my mind. Another day of 20 trips to the scale to see if that horrible number had gone down. Another day, where I would be half-alive in this world.

Though these descriptions seem so different, it's amazing how intertwined these two worlds really were. Each horrible pang of hunger, was power. Every time my heart would pound, and my chest would burn, I would feel alive. Every time I would wake up on the floor to realize I had fallen, I felt truly indestructible. Each muscle that would cramp and seize and send every sign for me to stop, I felt tough. I felt strong. I felt sure of something and myself, and that was something no one could take away from me.

I remember the life of lies, as if it were yesterday. "I just ate." "No, really, I'm not hungry." "I actually already made dinner plans," rolled off my tongue like they were truths. I think I may have even believed them. It's like my eating disorder ran me, controlled me, and even "looked out" for me. I pictured my eating disorder as a tiny person in my brain that pulled the strings on the body it had found home in. That voice, became my sounding board. "Can we eat this?" I'd ask. "You may run for even asking that," it would respond. And I would listen. The more I would listen, the quieter that disordered voice would be. But that's because it was winning. I just had to please it, and my day would go smoothly. Fall out of line and eat a big meal? Well, there were repercussions for that, and consequences to be suffered.

That disordered voice in my head would run through all of my viable options: "Can we purge at least? Has it been too long? The gym's still open for another hour... Looks like I'll restrict tomorrow to make up for this royal mess up." Life became a balancing act- of pleasing my eating disorder to its appropriate wishes and desires, while keeping it a secret from anyone possible. It loved its secrecy. I wasn't supposed to tell anyone about my eating disorder ride-along, because then they'd try to take it away. Little did I know, my "passenger" had already taken me.

I lost what it meant to be me. I lost what it felt like to feel something. I lost what it felt like to feel joy. All I knew was numbers, so many numbers. The calories, the weight, the miles, the minutes, the days, the carbs, the bites, the hours left before I earned my next bit of fuel... I was exhausted. I was hungry, and I was desperate. "Will I be like this forever?" Tomorrow was hard enough to face. "You're telling me there will be hundreds of thousands more tomorrows?"

Initially, each day was a battle. Each meal, was torture. Every bite, came more daunting than the last. I watched my friends and loved ones live their respective lives. Why didn't they feel the way I did? Why are they allowed to eat the cookies when I can't? Why did the food in their stomach get to stay there? How did they sleep knowing they barely exercised? I felt so far gone. The reality that I was watching of others? That wasn't possible for me. I could never be like them, I thought. I could never laugh while eating an immeasurable amount of ice cream. I could never smile while eating something that did not come with a nutrition label that passed my standards. That just wasn't in my cards.

I think what kept me in it for so long was the thought that I wouldn't actually die from this. I was in control. I had it, under control. Everyone kept saying I could die, but yet I kept waking up each morning. "If it gets that bad, I'll stop. It's not going to get that bad," I said to myself. I'm positive that I believed it. Then there came the day that I found out I would not save myself when death came knocking. If anything, I had chosen it. I had decided my only way out, was to get out: of here, the world, this Hell that had become my home.

I remember waking up in the hospital and setting out my arm out of habit so the nurse could take my vitals, a routine I had become used to during my time in treatment. It was in this moment that I realized, "What am I doing? Why am I doing this? Do I want more months of strangers watching me shower, sleep, and use the restroom?" That's not the reality I planned on. It's not a life I could live through again. I remember getting out of that hospital, determined not to waste another day in a gown. I knew this was my last chance. My friends and loved ones could not see me do this any longer. They had reached their end, while my path began to split. "Do I really throw in the towel? Do I let this disorder take the rest of me?

*Or do I – **try**?" I know that sounds like such a simple revelation, but this was the first moment where that word felt possible or applicable to me. "What did I do all of this for then if I give up on my disorder now? All of those hours and numbers and breakdowns were wasted?" Little did I know, those experiences were not wasted at all. That experience shaped who I am today and changed my life, and I know it can help change someone else's someday. I just took back the reins from the disorder that had controlled me for so long, and I did it on my time. I feel humbled to be here today, and grateful to have the chance to get hundreds of thousands more tomorrows. Though I don't know how many more there will be, I know one thing. I received a second chance on life that not everyone gets, and I don't intend to waste it.*

Reflection

It's quite interesting to reflect on that piece now. I know I could never have access to write it today. I'm grateful I took the time many years ago to reflect on it all from a recovery lens that was still relatively close in time to the disordered one. I don't think I realized then that this piece would almost function as a time capsule, as something that portrayed emotions that somehow would become more blurry with time. This shows just how far you can go.

If you can relate to anything in the story, I'm so sorry. Unfortunately, there are some sentiments that are far too common. If you can't relate but know someone who might, I hope you gleaned something new from it. If you are a provider, I hope you heard all that encompasses a life, not just the symptoms or the diagnosis. So much of these disorders, I don't believe can be read in a textbook; instead, they need to be shared through storytelling, experience, and connection.

If you're in the club that no one wants to be in, the one where your body or how you feed it consumes your life, please know there is an after. Coming from someone who believed for a very long time that there wouldn't be, I believe with my whole heart that individuals can come back to themselves; Don't let the eating disorder tell you otherwise.

Activities

Take what you like and leave what you don't. ☺ Everyone is different, and I acknowledge that not all of these may be fitting to your unique experience.

Reminder: *These activities are not intended to be therapeutic interventions. They are ideas that may be helpful in your journey of recovery, or in your work with individuals who are struggling. Please seek out professional resources; These are not intended to be stand-alone activities and are not intended to replace working with a professional.*

Some of these activities are not unique but instead widely used activities within the therapeutic community. Those established solely by Maria Ortiz will be marked with copyright.

Activities List: *Feel free to check them off as you go; You will find the activities in this chapter in this order on the remaining pages of the book. You got this!*

- o Positive Qualities
- o My Whys
- o Affirmations (Mirror)
- o My Circle
- o The Dinner Table
- o Things My ED Promised vs. Gave Me
- o Goals
- o Positive Pairing
- o Mindfulness
- o Prevention Plans
- o Bonfires
- o "If I Didn't Have An ED"
- o Draw
- o My Identity: The Real One
- o Letter to Your Body
- o Emotion Exploration
- o Letter to ED
- o Movement Exploration
- o Recovery Wins
- o Weekly Check-In

Positive Qualities

List positive qualities about your true self. Consider asking a trusted loved one or friend for a list about you as well. Read through the list on challenging days. Remember the things the ED wants you to forget.

○

○

○

○

○

○

○

○

○

○

○

○

○

○

○

○

○

○

○

<u>My Whys</u>

List the reasons you are fighting your eating disorder, and for your recovery and freedom.

(Examples: My health, to not feel controlled by food, to be present, etc.)

- ○
- ○
- ○
- ○
- ○
- ○
- ○
- ○
- ○
- ○
- ○
- ○
- ○
- ○
- ○
- ○
- ○
- ○

Affirmations (Mirror)

Write down some positive affirmations about yourself that challenge what your ED tries to say to you. Put them in the boxes below, then transfer onto sticky notes. Place the sticky notes on your mirror.

(Example: I am good enough the way I am, I am strong, etc.)

(Potential further step: Place them in locations intentionally to help prevent body-checking behaviors)

My Circle

Knowing who you can turn to matters. List the people in your life you can go to for support.

Disclaimer: Don't let your ED convince you that you either don't deserve support or are not worthy of reaching out for it. Remember: It is lying.

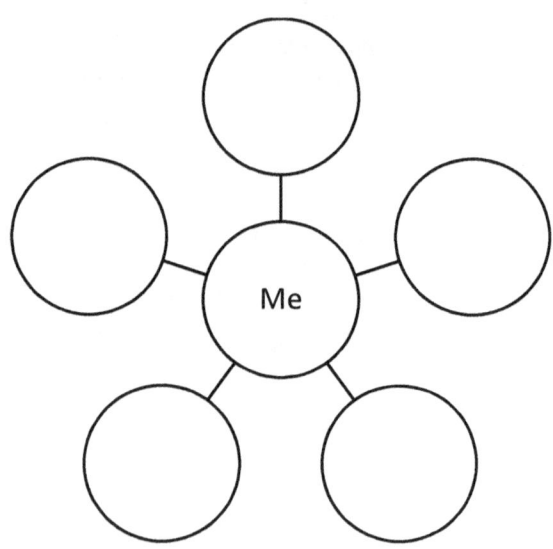

Who can you depend on the most? Why?

_____

_____

_____

The Dinner Table

Unfortunately for many individuals with an eating disorder, the dinner table can be a daunting place. If we have the capability to make this space more inviting, I typically recommend this. Below are a few examples of ways to embrace the dinner table in a recovery focused manner.

- o Make a placemat.
    - o Add photos, magazine clippings, favorite affirmations, motivating sentences, song lyrics, or all of your favorite colors to a piece of paper and laminate. Have a placemat under your plate that's intentional, rooted in your values, and recovery-oriented.
- o Make a table menu.
    - o Many restaurants have a small sign on their tables listing the specials, new arrivals, or the featured dish of the day. Get creative and make a little sign with a picture of your younger self. Put a quote below it encouraging them (younger you), saying that they're allowed to be happy and take care of themselves.
- o Get a new centerpiece. Set some flowers on the table. Set out a photo of your pet. Get a new coaster. Let yourself enjoy decorating your eating space.

Things My ED Promised vs. Gave Me

Circle any applicable experiences. Add in any that stand out for you. What does the ED __say__ it will give you?

Things My Eating Disorder *__Promised Me__*

Happiness	Safety	Comfort	Control	Weight loss	Positive body image
Feeling better	Less sadness	Better future	Other people caring	Sense of identity	Sense of achievement
Other Positives:					

Now that we've identified what the eating disorder has __said__ it will do for you, let's look at its __follow-through__. On the next page, circle any applicable experiences. Add in any that stand out for you.

Things My Eating Disorder *Actually Gave Me*

Happiness	Safety	Comfort	Control	Weight loss	Positive body image
Feeling better	Less sadness	Better future	Other people caring	Sense of identity	Sense of achievement
Other Positives:					

*What did the ED **follow through** on? Do these charts look the same or different?*

_____

_____

_____

_____

*Now that we've identified where the ED may or may not have followed through on its functional or "positive" promises, let's take a look at some of the **negatives** it may lead to on the next page as well. Circle any applicable experiences. Add in any that stand out for you.*

Things My Eating Disorder *Actually Gave Me*

Sadness	Insecurity	Sleep Issues	Took control of me	Still don't like my weight	Negative body image
Lack of self esteem	Discomfort	No energy	Inability to focus	Loss of friendships	Inability to feel happy
No hope	People still didn't care the way I wanted them to	Only identity is ED	Feeling worse	Inability to be present	Not enjoying things I used to like
More anxiety	Comparing my food/body to others around me	Only feeling numb	Not feeling good enough	Worse relationship with my body	Missing memories with friends and family
Other	**negatives:**				

What is your reaction to this activity? Did this shift any perspective?

_____

_____

_____

_____

_____

_____

_____

_____

_____

_____

_____

_____

Goals

What are you hoping to achieve in your recovery? List a few short-term (within a few weeks), intermediate-term (within a few months), and long-term (within a year or more) goals that you would like to meet. Highlight the ones that feel the most important to you.

Short Term:

- ○
- ○
- ○
- ○
- ○

Intermediate Term:

- ○
- ○
- ○
- ○
- ○

Long Term:

- ○
- ○
- ○
- ○
- ○

Positive Pairing

Purpose: The idea here is to identify what the brain responds well too; what is guaranteed to make you almost unintentionally crack a smile. Once we've identified what these stimuli look like, we engage with them while eating. The idea? Confuse the mind. Make it think, "Are we smiling and laughing while eating a fear food? Maybe we can smile and laugh when eating foods again?" This can look like listening to a favorite podcast, watching a favorite movie, or going to your favorite park while eating your meal or snack. As always, discuss with your provider before integrating.

Example: If you really enjoy watching a particular show, turn on the episode that has never failed to make you laugh during an exposure meal or snack. When the mind tries to send negative, fearful, or generally aversive thoughts due to presence of the fear food, the hope is for the positive stimulus to ignite some pleasure centers, balancing the experience to more neutral. This is most helpful combatting disorders where symptoms have an associated fear relating to eating food, due to amount, type, time, or potential "outcomes" from the intake.

What stimuli or circumstances in my life influence happy, cheerful, or comedic emotions for me?

_____

_____

_____

_____

_____

_____

_____

_____

_____

_____

_____

_____

_____

_____

_____

_____

_____

_____

_____

Mindfulness

Mindfulness can be so important for the mind-body connection while eating. Here are a few questions you can ask yourself before, during, or after eating to maintain connection and intention during mealtime.

Before

- o What am I hungry for?
- o How hungry am I?
- o Do I want something soft or crunchy?
- o Do I want something salty or sweet?
- o Are there any foods that have continued to sound yummy recently?
- o What is my body asking for?

During

- o How am I enjoying this meal?
- o Am I eating quickly or slowly?
- o Am I starting to get full?
- o Is this meal meeting my needs?
- o What is my favorite part of this meal?
- o Am I focused or distracted?

After

- o Am I satiated?
- o Do I feel hungry, full, or over-full?
- o Is that a meal I would have again?
- o Was this a meal I focused more on enjoyment or simply meeting needs?

Prevention Plan

Here is an example of a Prevention Plan that uses purging as the behavior to be prevented. You can insert/edit to fit a behavior you struggle with as needed.

My Purge Prevention Plan:

- o <u>Distract:</u> 5 things I can do
- o Examples:
    - o Paint nails
    - o Draw
    - o Schoolwork
    - o Journal
    - o Read a new book
- o <u>Acknowledge:</u> pathology vs. true thoughts *(Intentionally remember the ED is sending the urge; Not true self)*
- o <u>Write:</u> The harm purging has caused/can cause
- o <u>List:</u> 5 reasons that stand out why not to purge
- o <u>Support:</u> 2 people I can call/text
- o <u>Read:</u> 5 favorite affirmations
- o <u>Create space:</u> remove self from triggering environment *(stay away from the restroom)*
- o <u>Read:</u> letter to self *(written during neutral time in preparation for prevention plan)*

Bonfires

Each time you take a step towards recovery (conquer a fear food, say no to a strong urge, speak to yourself kindly, throw away old clothes, etc.), draw a log or a flame to build a *Recovery Bonfire*. Each time an ED urge wins, draw a log or a flame to make a *Disordered Bonfire* (do an act of self-care per item added to show self-compassion of meeting self where you are at).

Let's get that Recovery Bonfire shining bright!

Note: This activity is not meant to be shaming; it's meant to be intentional, increasing awareness of choices and behaviors, encouraging compassion on hard days, and highlighting the wins along the way.

Draw Below: Recovery Bonfire   Draw Below: Disordered Bonfire

"If I Didn't Have an Eating Disorder"

Journal Entry: If you were to wake up tomorrow without an ED, what would you do? How would you live differently? How would you feel? What would be the most significant changes?

_____

_____

_____

_____

_____

_____

_____

_____

_____

_____

_____

_____

_____

_____

Draw

On this page, draw what it feels like to be deep in an eating disorder. On the next page, draw what recovery feels like.

No judgment of self on perceptions/art themes/portrayals.

Life in an Eating Disorder:

Life in Recovery

<u>My Identity: The Real One</u>

Tell me all about yourself. No, I don't just mean the more obvious identities like student, mom, brother, athlete, etc. Write about your quirks, your secret fears, your funniest moments, your goals you keep quiet, the items in your home you can't get rid of, how many alarms you set each day...

The things that truly make you, you.

_____

_____

_____

_____

_____

_____

_____

_____

_____

_____

Letter to Your Body

Write a letter to your body. Depending on where you're at in your recovery, the tone and message will look different. Include a greeting and sign-off.

_____

_____

_____

_____

_____

_____

_____

_____

_____

_____

_____

_____

_____

_____

_____

Emotion Exploration

What emotions am I most likely to push down, numb, or try to get rid of quickly?

_____

_____

_____

What emotions am I most comfortable with experiencing?

_____

_____

_____

How comfortable and confident am I with navigating my emotions?

(10 being most comfortable/confident)

1 2 3 4 5 6 7 8 9 10

What did my family of origin teach me about emotions? How were different emotions expressed and viewed growing up?

_____

_____

_____

_____

What emotions do I experience most frequently? How do I feel about this?

_____

_____

_____

_____

_____

What emotions do I struggle to feel, or less often experience fully?

_____

_____

_____

_____

_____

Have I ever been shamed for experiencing any of my emotions? How has this influenced my perception of them?

_____

_____

_____

_____

_____

Do I fake any emotions? If so, why?

_____

_____

_____

_____

How do my emotions influence my relationship with food, eating, and my body?

_____

_____

_____

_____

_____

_____

How do food, eating, and my body influence my emotions?

_____

_____

_____

_____

_____

_____

Letter to ED

Write a letter to your eating disorder. Depending on where you're at in your recovery, the tone and message will look different. Include a greeting and sign-off.

_____

_____

_____

_____

_____

_____

_____

_____

_____

_____

_____

_____

_____

_____

Movement Exploration

If there was no chance at all that my body would change
(weight/body composition wise), what exercise/movement
would I engage with often? Why?

_____

_____

_____

_____

If I'm engaging with exercise/movement right now, what are
my motivations behind it?

_____

_____

_____

_____

What kind of relationship would I like to have with exercise?
What changes would I make from the one I have today?

_____

_____

_____

_____

What sort of exercise or movement makes me feel connected to my body and its sensations?

_____

_____

_____

_____

What sort of exercise or movement makes me feel disconnected from my body and its sensations?

_____

_____

_____

_____

What language have I heard around what constitutes something as exercise? Did people model that walking is wonderful movement, or encourage more intense exercise? How does this shape how I engage with my body?

_____

_____

_____

_____

<u>Recovery Wins</u>

List the progress that you have made in recovery so far.

(Examples: Increased intake, ceased/lessened ED behaviors,

improved body image, more engagement with life outside ED, etc.)

- o
- o
- o
- o
- o
- o
- o
- o
- o
- o
- o
- o
- o
- o
- o
- o
- o

Weekly Check In

One week from the Coming Back to Myself Workbook. Complete while reflecting upon previous week.

Week 1

Date:

Emotion Word Describing Week:

_____

Why did you choose the word that you did? Explain.

_____

_____

_____

_____

_____

Did you take intentional steps to meet your goals last week?

Yes   No   (Circle one)

If yes, list the steps you are most proud of yourself for.

- ○

- ○

- ○

- ○

- ○

If no, list a self-care step you can engage with immediately following this activity today to show yourself kindness and compassion, even on weeks you feel you didn't meet your goals.

_____

_____

My overall rating of my week is (Circle one, 10 being the best)

1 2 3 4 5 6 7 8 9 10

Why did you choose the number that you did? Explain.

_____

_____

_____

_____

What would've made this week better?

_____

_____

_____

_____

My high(s)/win(s) this week was/were:

○

○

○

○

My low(s)/challenge(s) this week was/were:

- ○
- ○
- ○
- ○

Something I'd like support on from my providers/loved ones this week is:

_____

_____

_____

_____

Today's motivators for recovery are:

- ○
- ○
- ○

My goal for next week is:

_____

_____

_____

_____

Intentional steps I can take to meet my goal are:

_____

_____

_____

_____

A recovery-focused affirmation I'd like to focus on this week is:

_____

_____

_____

Keep fighting. You deserve to Come Back to Yourself.

More Resources:

Email: mortiz@breakfreetherapyservices.com to be added to the email list for notification of further releases from the author.

Recommended reading:

Coming Back To Myself

The Workbook: Finding My Freedom One Week at a Time

What's next from the author?

Grace over Guilt: A Faithful Path to Food Freedom

This new release will again be a blend of lived experience and professional perspective, examining the relationship between an individual's Faith and their eating disorder, and how this impacts the recovery process.

www.ingramcontent.com/pod-product-compliance
Lightning Source LLC
Chambersburg PA
CBHW020739130626
46554CB00006B/2057